30 Devo
WOMEN IN BUSINESS

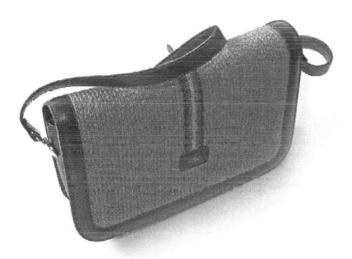

Maggie White

TheBiblePeople.com

30 Devotions for Women in Business

© 2012 TheBiblePeople.com

Published by TheBiblePeople.com. Our mission is to encourage people to read, understand, and apply the Bible.

Printed in the United States of America.

CONTENTS

READING ONE

Bringing God's Light Into the Office

"You are the light of the world. A city that is set on a hill cannot be hidden. Nor do they light a lamp and put it under a basket, but on a lampstand and it gives light to all who are in the house. Let your light so shine before men, that they may see your good works and glorify your Father in Heaven." Matthew 5:14-16 (KJV)

SOMEONE at work once told me, "You bring such sunshine in with you each day." My coworkers saw that sunshine in the form of smiles and kind words. They saw me as a cheerful, uplifting spirit that came into the office with an upbeat, "Good morning". God created us to be a light unto the world. He created us to be joy and happiness for others. We have been sent out into our respective places of business to shine God's light. We bring prayer into businesses, Godly ways into negotiations, a spirit of goodwill into an office of potentially selfish colleagues, and a feeling of happiness to those who might otherwise be experiencing tough times. As we go into the workplace, remember that we are bringing light. We are bringing hope. We are, in effect, bringing God into the way we accomplish our business. We do not need to necessarily quote a scripture; we may simply smile, be a positive force, or say a kind word, and others will feel that "goodness" that we bring and they will gravitate to it. As they do, they gravitate toward our Heavenly Father.

God, we thank you for the opportunity to be salt and light to the world. God we thank you that others will see you through us – through our behavior, our attitude, our kind words, and our smiles. God, we thank you for an opportunity to be a ray of hope for someone else in an environment where many do not expect to see you. God, we thank you that this day, someone will experience your light and your love through us. Thank you, Lord, for using us this day. Amen.

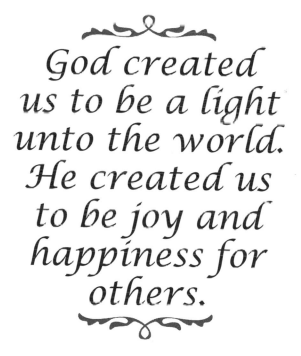

God created
us to be a light
unto the world.
He created us
to be joy and
happiness for
others.

READING TWO

Fulfilling Our Dreams

"Blessed is she who believes that the Lord will fulfill his promises to her." Luke 1:45 (NIV)

WE all have dreams inside of us. Those dreams are placed inside of us by our Heavenly Father. We naturally possess the skills to excel when we use God's gifts. God's gifts are not simply for us to use at home or in our places of worship. God's gifts extend to the workplace and to our careers. Many of us desire to do things outside of the scope of what we have already been doing. For those of us who work on a team, we may desire to lead a team or even become the manager of a project. Managers may desire to grow in various skill sets, or even get promoted to a higher managing position. Some may even desire to branch out and start a new small business. We must not be afraid of taking the next steps

9

in our careers, or even changing careers or professions. God has promised to bless the woman who believes that he will fulfill his promises to her. When God directs our hearts (even in the area of our professions), we must step out with faith and believe that we can and will achieve whatever God desires and plans for us.

Dear Heavenly Father, we thank you today for blessing our aspirations. God, we pray for the strength and the faith to step out and do what you have given us the tools to do. We thank you, God, because we serve a limitless God who says that we can do all things. We thank you helping us to accept your Word and your promises. Lord, please guide us in our next steps as we draw closer to your purposes for all areas of our lives. In Jesus' name we pray. Amen.

When God directs our hearts (even in the area of our professions), we must step out with faith and believe that we can and will achieve whatever God desires and plans for us.

READING THREE

Avoiding Water Cooler Negativity

"Avoid godless chatter, because those who indulge in it will become more and more ungodly." 2 Timothy 2:16 (NIV)

BEFORE the Keurig, we used to stand around the water cooler, where the office "gossip" occurred. Now we may engage in negative conversation near the kitchen as we make our single-serve coffee, on the walk downstairs to the cafeteria, or even leaning in the doorway of our office or cubical.

Speaking negatively about how our Program Manager is taking the project in the wrong direction, or about how the finance department continues to overprice our bids is still godless chatter, even if we feel these things to be true. Do these conversations help our office or company grow? Do they help promote better cost models for pricing? Do they provide the Program Manager suggestions on how to redirect the project?

The answer is "no". Anything that does not uplift is godless chatter. Participating in it (even listening) will take us in the opposite direction on our road to becoming more and more like Christ.

Dear God, help us to refrain from conversation that does not uplift and inspire. God, it is so easy to fall into either engaging in this type of conversation or listening to it, but we ask for self-control. God, if there is any way that we can support areas of our businesses that have room for growth, let us contribute positively through helpful suggestions or advice. God, we thank you that today we have been made aware of our actions, and we commit to doing better in this area. Amen.

Anything
that does
not uplift is
godless chatter.
Participating
in it (even
listening) will
take us in
the opposite
direction on
our road to
becoming more
and more like
Christ.

READING FOUR

Take a Break

"Six days thou shalt work, but on the seventh day thou shalt rest: even during the plowing season and harvest you must rest." Exodus 34:21 (NIV)

L IKE everything else on the earth, God created rest. This is not meant to stifle us but to give us recovery – mentally, physically, and spiritually. As women, we often work at home; we care for parents, family, children, and friends; we serve in ministry; *and* we give 200% in our careers. When do we rest?

Do we continue starting early and finishing late each day to win new business, maintain current business, meet with clients, and respond to countless emails without recovering? Many of us do. God appreciates our diligence and our desire for excellence, but it is when we slow down mentally, physically, and spiritually, that we can truly hear from God. In today's business world, the 9 to 5 work day does not exist. Work bleeds over into every hour of the day, but God has provided us rest if only we would choose to accept it. Rest will cause the cells of our bodies to renew; but more importantly, our spirit will renew as well. As we set about our day, striving to accomplish goals in our careers and setting out to be responsive to our managers and our clients, let us carve out some time to enjoy the beautiful gift of rest.

Dear God, right now we exhale. We thank you for this moment of rest and peace. God, we welcome your rest. God, tonight we curl up with you – we clear our mind of deadlines, of responsibilities, of time management, and even tomorrow's calendar. Tonight we give pause and let you revive us and renew us. We thank you that we serve a God that desires our renewal. Thank you for rest. Thank you for sweet sleep. Amen.

Work bleeds over into every hour of the day, but God has provided us rest if only we would choose to accept it.

READING FIVE

Growth Takes Time

"Do not be anxious about anything, but in everything by prayer and petition, with thanksgiving, present your requests to God." Philippians 4:6 (NIV)

BUSINESSES take time to grow. Developing relationships with new clients, writing proposals, and even having the internal infrastructure to support business growth, take time. However, we live in the age of instant gratification. We are like the little girl in *Willy Wonka and the Chocolate Factory* that wanted the golden goose and sang, "I want it now!" Willy Wonka didn't listen to the little girl's impatient demand, and God doesn't cater to our every desire, either. While it is understandable to desire growth of the company or a department, clients, contracts, and revenue, God wants us to be his patient children, trusting that he will provide for us according to his divine knowledge of what is good, and he will provide it at the appropriate time. God is like a parent who wants to give his children the desires of their heart, but first he must make sure that we can handle what we are asking for, or if we still need time to mature.

In desiring growth, trust that God hears our prayers, is paying attention, and is working things out for us for the most divine moment. Faith is the substance of things hoped for, and the evidence of things unseen, so we must exercise faith in our prayers. God's bountiful blessings have already been ordained for us.

Dear Heavenly Father, we thank you that we are not anxious about tomorrow. God, because we have been diligent in our actions and in our prayer and supplication to you, we know that you are working everything out on our behalf. God, we thank you for what is about to occur next. We thank you for future development, growth, and new positioning. Lord, we know that when growth comes, we will be ready. Amen.

In desiring
growth, trust
that God hears
our prayers,
is paying
attention, and
is working
things out
for us for the
most divine
moment.

READING SIX

Celebrate Even the Losses

"Rejoice always, pray continually, give thanks in all circumstances; for this is God's will for you in Christ Jesus."
1 Thessalonians 5:16-18 (NIV)

CHAMPAGNE toasts signify the winning of new business. Have you had a champagne toast recently in your business, or are you awaiting news that one of your proposals will be selected for a project award? The world tells us to celebrate winning, and to celebrate when we get what we want. Jesus teaches us to celebrate all things. God tells us to rejoice always – no matter what. Rejoice and continue to pray, even when things don't go our way. Submitting proposal after proposal and not receiving awards can begin to affect our faith. It is, after all, the way our businesses remain operational, but God asks us to just trust his will for us. We still need to remember to give thanks when it does not seem like we received our desired outcome.

Dear God, we want to thank you right now for every circumstance. God, we rejoice today, even though it may not be easy or seem as if we have much to rejoice about. Lord, we rejoice because you are still in charge. Lord, we thank you even for our proposal losses. God, we will submit our proposals to you first in prayer, and thank you in advance for whatever decision we receive. God, replace any lack of faith and any disappointment with thanks, praise, and trust in you. Amen.

We still need
to remember
to give thanks
when it does
not seem like
we received
our desired
outcome.

READING SEVEN

Trusting God in a Weak Economy

"Even strong young lions sometimes go hungry, but those who trust in the Lord will lack no good thing." Psalm 34:10 (NLT)

IN a time when businesses are going under, sales are down, and companies are laying off employees, it is easy to become concerned. We get concerned about whether or not our contract will end and our management services will no longer be needed. We get anxious about receiving a pay cut. We even get concerned about possibly needing to give the disappointing news to a subordinate that they will be laid off.

It is a fact that these things do happen. They are a part of this world of business that we live and often thrive in. The awesome thing about God is that because we put our full trust in him and we follow his commands, we will not lack any good thing. We may not be a strong lion, but in him, we, the weak are *made* strong. When we see a co-worker packing up her things, or hear that a client has cancelled their contract with the company, we must speak to our nervousness and our anxiety and remind ourselves that, because we trust in the Lord, we will lack no good thing.

God, we thank you this day for your provisions in the midst of economic downturn and stagnation. God, we thank you that you protect us always. God, we put our trust in you this day, looking not to the left or right to see what is going on around us, but looking up to you. Thank you for protecting our position, our financial resources, and our team. Amen.

The awesome
thing about
God is that
because we put
our full trust
in him and
we follow his
commands, we
will not lack
any good thing.

READING EIGHT

Praying for Difficult Colleagues and Clients

"I urge, then, first of all that requests, prayers, intercession and thanksgiving be made for everyone." 1 Timothy 2:1 (NIV)

HAVE you ever had to deal with difficult clients, or even co-workers? It is almost inevitable. It is natural when so many different personalities come together. Like the Tower of Babel, it almost seems like we are speaking different languages. Really, we are not; we simply have different vantage points, experiences, communication styles, and opinions. Some co-workers or clients appear to be antagonistic, moody, or even rude in terms of how they communicate. When this occurs, let us remember to think and act like Christ. We do not know what is going on in the lives of our clients or our co-workers. We do not know the state of their marriages, the health of their parents, or their financial obligations. When communication is trying, let us not respond negatively (in our minds or out loud). Instead, let us pray for them, their circumstances, our interaction with them, and the project that we are trying to accomplish. It really does help.

Dear God, help us to refrain from negative thoughts and negative words when dealing with difficult co-workers and clients. God, rather than speaking to who they seem to be, help us to speak to who they can be in you. Help us to speak to whatever may be going on in their lives. Lord, let us also take a moment to pray about what we may be doing to cause that reaction. Lord, it is not about us. In every interaction, it is about you. God, help us to pray and intercede for all those we interact with, regardless of whether or not we have an amicable relationship. Amen.

*When
communication
is trying, let
us not respond
negatively
(in our minds
or out loud).
Instead, let us
pray for them.*

READING NINE

Recognizing Others

"Great are your purposes and mighty are your deeds. Your eyes are open to the ways of all mankind; you reward each person according to their conduct and as their deeds deserve." Jeremiah 32:19 (NIV)

PERFORMANCE reviews occur annually, or sometimes semi-annually, but is that often enough to really recognize our hard work? God appreciates the contributions we make to his kingdom every day. Do we do that for our team, our colleagues, and support staff? We often get so caught up in the bottom line that we neglect to appreciate the contributions of our team and colleagues that directly support our success. Some people may simply do the bare minimum; however, what about the countless others that go above and beyond daily? What about the others that stay at the office until 4 am to complete the proposal that is due by noon the next day? What about the team member that finalizes a report from her hospital bed because the team is counting on her?

These people may work for us, or they may be a member of the team, but let us recognize their deeds and let us appreciate the willing spirit they maintain as they do these things. Let us appreciate the person from another department that pitches in on our own team when their project is slow. Their help is of great value, so let us show them. A kind word of appreciation, accolades in the company newsletter, or even a nice lunch or cup of coffee can mean so much.

Lord, help us to be mindful of the contributions of others. Lord, let us not wait until an annual performance review or peer review to tell someone "thank you" and appreciate their efforts and their willingness to go the extra mile. God, we thank you today that you are an example to us in all areas. God, we pray that we can look more like you each time we reward positive deeds and a positive attitude. Amen.

God appreciates the contributions we make to his kingdom every day. Do we do that for our team, our colleagues, and support staff?

READING TEN

Being Patient with Internal Processes

"But for that very reason I was shown mercy so that in me, the worst of sinners, Christ Jesus might display his unlimited patience as an example for those who would believe in him and receive eternal life." 1 Timothy 1:16 (NIV)

EACH and every day we go into the office, God provides us with unlimited opportunities to exhibit patience. Be it a large bureaucratic organization with red tape and cumbersome internal processes, or a small organization with little to no organization and established processes; both can be completely frustrating if you allow them to be. In both types of organizations, those challenges can make it seemingly difficult to get things accomplished at times, but it is in our most frustrating moments that we can display Christ-like temperance and patience. When we run into moments where our ability to move forward at the rate that we desire is hindered, let us be reminded of the patience Jesus Christ shows to even the worst sinners.

Heavenly Father, we take a deep breath and we release our frustration to you. We ask that you would replace our frustrations with patience. In doing so, God, we know that we will inspire patience from others as well. God, let us seek to be the change in our organizations, rather than one of the complainers. We thank you that you are patient with us and so we propel that patience forward. Amen.

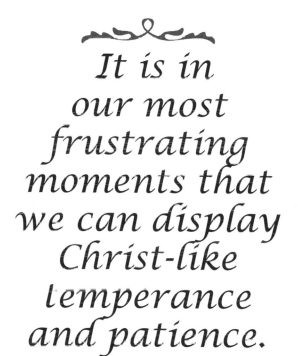

It is in our most frustrating moments that we can display Christ-like temperance and patience.

READING ELEVEN

Presenting with Confidence

"But blessed is the man who trusts in the LORD, whose confidence is in Him." Jeremiah 17:7 (NIV)

PUBLIC speaking can be one of the scariest things to do. Many studies even show that people fear public speaking more than death, yet it is something that we have to do more and more as we grow in our careers. Presentations for clients meetings, presentations to upper management, and oral presentations where the team presents its proposal to the selection committee can all cause great anxiety. Rather than being anxious and speaking a spirit of nervousness into the atmosphere, we should submit our presentation to the Lord. When we prepare fully and practice our presentation, we can confidently pray over that presentation and know that, because we have done our part, God will take care of the rest.

Dear God, we commit our upcoming presentation to you. Because we have prepared and been diligent, we know that you will bless the rest. God, we pray that you would order the words that come out of our mouths -- that you would create fluid diction, free of any stammering, and leave us poised with confidence. God, we pray to exude a peace that passes all understanding. God, we thank you for the best presentation we have ever given to date. Amen.

Rather than
being anxious
and speaking
a spirit of
nervousness
into the
atmosphere,
we should
submit our
presentation to
the Lord.

READING TWELVE

Learning from Others

"Listen to advice and accept discipline, and at the end you will be counted among the wise." Proverbs 19:20 (NIV)

WHEN we enter the world of work, we tend to be very open to advice. Some would say that new professionals are green, bright-eyed, and ready to learn. As the years go on and the responsibilities and accomplishments grow, it is easy to forget that we do not know everything and that we all must be held accountable to someone else. Managers report to Directors. Directors report to Vice Presidents. Presidents even report to shareholders and the Board.

We are not an island. We are only as good as those that surround us. Those around us (regardless of their place on the organizational chart) have wisdom to share, as we all have different experiences. We have worked with different clients and on different projects, each with their own set of nuances. Listening to the lessons learned from our colleagues makes us wise, and they make our work more efficient. Listening to others leads to cost savings, time savings, and efficient use of resources.

Dear Heavenly Father, thank you for reminding us that we do not know it all, nor do we need to. We thank you for your wisdom. We thank you for the wisdom and advice of others. God, we ask you to help us to humbly accept discipline. God, we pray that we would be slow to speak and quick to listen. God, we pray that we would not just hear advice and discipline, but that we would heed it. We thank you, God, for being the first and highest Project Management Professional. We thank you for placing directions for us in your Word that teach us the best ways for managing. God, you know about being on time and on budget, and you give us best practices even in your Word. Please help us to create an atmosphere where all team members are comfortable sharing experiences which may lead to the betterment of all organizational goals. Thank you, God, for using the experience of others to make us better. Amen.

We are not an
island. We are
only as good
as those that
surround us.

READING THIRTEEN

Write to Win

"Do you not know that in a race all the runners run, but only one gets the prize? Run in such a way as to get the prize." 1 Corinthians 9:24 (NIV)

GOD says to be awesome! God says to be excellent! Run the race to win -- do not simply run. After writing proposal after proposal, it is easy to get into the habit of cutting and pasting content and making sure that we are simply meeting the criteria. Will that lead to a win? Usually the answer is "no". This is a race, a race for new business and maybe a brand new client. Cutting and pasting to simply meet the criteria makes you one of the runners who just runs without the intent to win the race and get the prize. Next time your firm responds to a request for a proposal, think through the needs of the client, think through an approach that stands out and provides innovation beyond simply what is being asked for, and make the proposal personal to that potential client. In other words, write not for the sake of just writing, but write in such a way to get the prize.

Thank you, God, for your Word today. Thank you for making it directly applicable to what we experience in our office settings. Thank you for providing us counsel in every area of our work – even guidance for writing proposals. God, as we set out to write our next proposal, we purpose to follow your standards and write for the sake of winning the prize. God, help us to write in such a way to exceed the requirements. Help us write to supply an outstanding approach. We thank you, God, because if we do as you command and apply your Word, you will bless the work of our hands. Amen.

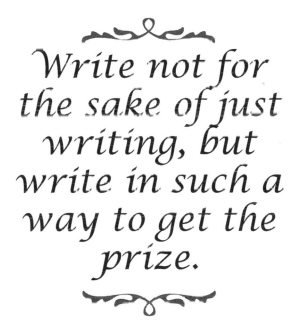

Write not for
the sake of just
writing, but
write in such a
way to get the
prize.

READING FOURTEEN

Keep the Schedule

"But whoever keeps his word, in him truly the love of God is perfected. By this we may know that we are in him." 1 John 2:5 (NIV)

IN these days of project management accountability, most projects are governed by a plan: a schedule that says what will be provided, when, and by whom. When we develop our project plans, we should make it a point to drive the project in that direction. After all, this is what we promised our clients, and we owe them our best efforts to deliver. Maintaining our project schedules is not always easy. It requires cooperation from various resources and dedication from a team of professionals. It requires strong leadership, which is not always comfortable, but it is our duty as managers to keep things on track as much as possible. It is our responsibility to let clients and other vendors know what dependencies we have and what support we need from them. We must manage our contracts by God's principals. Our schedule is our word – let's commit to keeping it. When we keep our word, we exemplify Christ.

Dear God, we thank you this morning for our integrity. We thank you, God, for the opportunity to be like you in all things. This morning, we recommit ourselves to managing our projects like God. We commit to doing what we promised to do for our clients. Amen.

Our schedule is our word – let's commit to keeping it. When we keep our word, we exemplify Christ.

READING FIFTEEN

Written Commitments

"Men swear by someone greater than themselves, and the oath confirms what is said and puts an end to all argument." Hebrews 6:16 (NIV)

DOING business with other firms can be delicate. They said one thing, and we said another thing, but we may think that we are both saying the same thing. God knew what many of us have come to learn over time – we need an oath: a document, an agreement that confirms that we are all on the same page. It is so amazing that God knew all about business even before the first organization was incorporated. God knew that we needed Non-Disclosure Agreements, Offer Letters, and Teaming Agreements. These agreements keep business relationships away from discord. God hates discord and loves agreement.

Dear God, let us not forget to set up written agreements when conducting business. God, have us remember to clearly communicate in writing what we desire and what we expect. God, we thank you for giving us all that we need to manage and run our businesses your way. Thank you for thinking of what we would need even before we came into being. God, we thank you that your Word is relevant in every aspect of our business and professions. Thank you for being an amazing God. Amen.

It is so amazing that God knew all about business even before the first organization was incorporated.

READING SIXTEEN

The Sky is the Limit

"Now faith is being sure of what we hoped for and certain of what we do not see. This is what the ancients were commended for. By faith we understand that the universe was formed at God's command, so that what is seen was not made out of what was visible." Hebrews 11:1-3 (NIV)

WHEN we start out in business, we do not know where we will go or what we will accomplish. We cannot see that far ahead. When we start out as entry-level Analysts, we have no idea if we will end up being a Project Manager, Chief Operations Officer, Head of Marketing, or the Chief Executive Officer. Even though we do not know where we will end up, faith is knowing that we will end up in one of those positions, if that is what we desire and work towards. We do not always know how we will get from one role to another, but with faith, time, and hard work, it can happen. For those of us who have already experienced seeing our faith come to fruition, let us thank God today that his Word has been true.

Dear God, thank you for our faith that you will give us what we cannot see, simply because we believe. God, we thank you for the opportunities that you give us that lead us to our future growth. Today we commit our faith to you that we would grow from the role that we are in right now to the role that you have prepared for us. Let us never believe that it is impossible, even though we cannot see it; instead, let us know that by your command it will come to be. Amen.

We do not
always know
how we will
get from one
role to another,
but with faith,
time, and hard
work, it can
happen.

READING SEVENTEEN

Business – A Woman's World, Too

"A kind-hearted woman gains respect, but ruthless men gain only wealth." Proverbs 11:16 (NIV)

THERE was a time when people thought that women had to be ruthless in order to survive in the world of business, a world previously thought to be a "man's world". God knew what many of us are only recently realizing; women do not have to imitate the actions of men in business in order to be successful. In fact, as women, we have a certain kindness and finesse that we bring to engagements, that men often lack. While ruthless men gain only wealth, the kind-hearted woman can gain both respect and wealth.

Clients appreciate a kind-hearted woman's sensitivity and empathy to their project needs. Clients appreciate a woman's ability to identify with their issues and concerns, and put them at ease. That respect and that relationship can yield huge dividends later. We must not be afraid to let our feminine characteristics and traits shine through. God says that we are wonderfully made (just as He made us). That extends to our business.

Lord, thank you for encouraging us to be the women you designed us to be in the office. Thank you, God, that we do not have to resemble a man in order to be successful. Thank you for giving us characteristics that are specifically beneficial to this purpose. Lord, today we appreciate who you made us. We pray that our kindness would be a benefit to our clients, and that we develop relationships that extend beyond the current engagement to many others in the future. Amen.

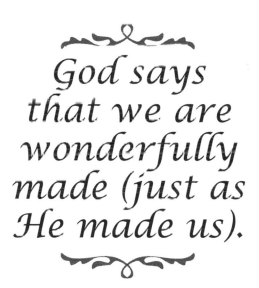

God says
that we are
wonderfully
made (just as
He made us).

READING EIGHTEEN

Networking 101

"Be wise in the way that you act with outsiders; make the most of every opportunity." Colossians 4:5 (NIV)

EACH interaction we have can lead to an opportunity in the future. Many of us attend networking functions specifically designed to meet potential teaming companies, new employees, and also organizations that may need the services or products that we provide. Realize that every interaction we have with another person is a form of networking. The impression that you make with that person will determine if you interact with them again. Someone you interact with in the halls of your company's building may research your company and ask you to join their team, or may solicit your company's service, based solely on what they experienced during your interaction with them. We should be mindful to always exemplify knowledge about our industry, integrity, and a positive attitude.

Lord, we thank you for this nugget of wisdom. God, we sit in awe of you once more. You knew about networking when there was no such word to describe it. Dear God, in all of our interactions, we will remember to conduct ourselves properly- never knowing how our paths with others may cross again. God, we thank you because you are the author and the one who predestines our opportunities. In all that we do, in every interaction with each person, order our actions; have them be an example of our ethical and godly business practices. Let others see something in us that would facilitate an opportunity in the future. Amen.

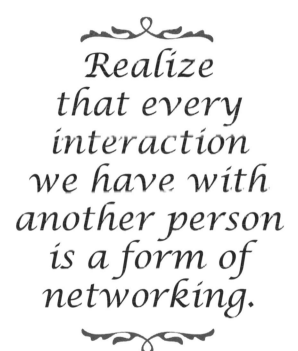

*Realize
that every
interaction
we have with
another person
is a form of
networking.*

READING NINETEEN

Being Honest is Being Transparent

"They did not require an accounting from those to whom they gave the money to pay the workers, because they acted with complete honesty." 2 Kings 12:15 (NIV)

CLIENTS expect their contractors to be honest with them. Honesty is not always an easy pill for clients to swallow; nor is it easy for contractors to present, but in the long run it promotes a healthy work environment. Some conversations are difficult, but also critical and necessary. When we do not share risks with clients, or tell them that a certain dependency is holding up the progress of the work, we only create confusion and distrust, and we open the door for a negative client relationship.

Clients prefer when we share risks early (when they are just risks, not disasters). When we put this conversation off until risks become issues, that is where the real problem arises. Be honest! Be transparent! When we are transparent, our clients will not attempt to micromanage the details of the project, because they have full confidence in us to manage the work. Be the manager who is honest. Be a trusted partner.

Dear God, we thank you today for an honest spirit. We thank you for the fearlessness to communicate difficult conversations and risks to customers early on. Lord, help us to be transparent with our clients, even when it may cause concerns or anxiety. Lord, help us to better represent you in our business relationships. God, we commit ourselves to being to be more attentive to risks early in our projects, and to communicate them long before they become actual issues. God, thank you for reminding us not to make promises that we know we cannot keep. God, thank you for showing us how to have better client relationships and how to create atmospheres of trust. Amen.

Honesty is not always an easy pill for clients to swallow; nor is it easy for contractors to present, but in the long run it promotes a healthy work environment.

READING TWENTY

It's Not About Us

"Do nothing out of selfish ambition or vain conceit, but in humility consider others better than yourselves. Each of you should look not only to your own interests, but also to the interests of others. Your attitude should be the same as that of Christ Jesus." Philippians 2:3-5 (NIV)

WORKING in a team environment has become increasingly popular. Probably 90 percent of us would say that we work with a team to some capacity. Teams require collaboration: consideration of others' interests and ideas. Sometimes being on a team means being humble and putting others first. It has to be about the team and not the individual. As human beings, we seem to be innately selfish, but God says that we are to be humble.

How many times do we come into a team meeting with our own agenda, not at all concerned about the agendas of others? How many times do we want to get kudos for what we as the individual accomplished, instead of sharing the spotlight for that accomplishment with the entire team, because we feel that we were the major contributor to the team's success? How many times have we put our individual wants and desires above the organization's goals and strategic vision? Without collaboration and consideration for the company as a whole, as well as other colleagues, the business cannot grow. That means that we as individuals can't grow, either. In the future, we must be less self-centered and more organization-centered. Watch how much further the business (and we) will go!

Dear God, we thank you for the team as a whole. God, we thank you for each of our co-workers, and we ask to become more interested in the agenda of the team. God, we pray to become better team players; to think less of ourselves and more about furthering the pursuits of our organization. God, we ask for an attitude of Christ. Help us to have a servant heart like yours; a heart that knows how to put itself last so that others can be first. Be with us, God, as we begin our journey to humility. May our advances be seen throughout our office and be exemplified in our conduct. In Jesus' name. Amen.

Sometimes being on a team means being humble and putting others first. It has to be about the team and not the individual.

READING TWENTY-ONE

Living with a Plan

"Then the Lord replied: 'Write down the revelation and make it plain on tablets so that a herald may run with it." Habakkuk 2:2 (NIV)

WHAT do you want to accomplish this week, this month, or even today? What are your goals in your career, with your team, on your projects, or in your company? Do you know? Have you given it any thought? We should. We should not only think about it, but the Bible tells us to *write it down*. Make a plan and make it clear. We cannot know what we aim for until we set a target. When we set a target, it is far more likely that we will reach it. We do not know if we have made our sales goals if we do not set projections. We will not know who we will sell to if we do not plan who we will prospect. How will others know the plan if it is only in our head? How will they interpret a plan that is still in the conception stages of our mind? How then can we measure what we have accomplished?

Thank you, God, for knowing just what we need. We thank you for your instruction. God, You said that we should write down our vision and make it plain, so today we write it down. God, today, please lead us to a place where we plan our path forward; a place where we write down the vision of our organization and our team. Today, we mediate on those things that we desire to accomplish. Lord, our lives and days become so hectic that it is easy to veer away from the path of the vision, but today we heed your advice. This day, we write our plans down clearly, we pray over them, and we seek your direction in each step.

Make a plan
and make
it clear. We
cannot know
what we aim
for until we set
a target.

READING TWENTY-TWO

Listening to Our Clients

"He who answers before listening - that is his folly and his shame." Proverbs 18:13 (NIV)

HOW many times do we go into a client meeting with prescriptions for the issue before really listening to the concern? So many times we assume that we know what a client wants or needs, and we never really take the time to inquire from and listen to the client. If we do not hear the issue from them, how can we come close to solving the problem? It is so important to get to know our clients – even, and especially, early on in the relationship. Take time to find out what their challenges are, where they need innovation, how much they can and want to spend, and their priorities. Doing so allows us to provide the best service possible; service that keeps them coming back for more.

Heavenly Father, we thank you for another opportunity to infuse your wisdom into our daily lives. We thank you, God, that you provide wisdom in the Scriptures that we can apply to every area of our lives. Lord, we desire to provide the best service to our clients; service that really speaks to their needs. God, going forward, we will listen before making assumptions. We will listen in such a way to truly hear what is being said. God, incline our ears to hear first and try to solve problems later. We pray that we will not continue to offer our clients solutions to problems that we think they have, but that we will provide solutions to the problems they know they have. Amen.

*It is so
important to
get to know
our clients—
even, and
especially,
early on in the
relationship.*

READING TWENTY-THREE

Everyone Deserves Respect

"Give everyone what you owe him: If you owe taxes, pay taxes; if revenue, then revenue; if respect, then respect; if honor, then honor." Romans 13:7 (NIV)

REGARDLESS of whether we agree with the direction a manager takes the team, the knowledge of the manager on the task, or even the manager's ability to lead that project, we owe respect where respect is due. Supervisors do not always know the right answers or the right actions to take, but because they are in a role of authority, they deserve our respect. If we disagree with their approach, we must pray for them that God would order their steps and their actions. We must pray that they would utilize the knowledge on the team and use the expertise around them. What we must not do is be disrespectful.

In fact, everyone deserves our respect. Everyone deserves to be heard in a meeting if they opt to speak. Everyone deserves to be spoken to with a professional tone. Let us respect our managers and our colleagues as God requires.

Dear God, we pray that you would change our attitude if we are being disrespectful. Create in us a clean heart and renew a right spirit in us. God, we desire to give honor and respect to all around us. We desire to follow your commands. God, it is our prayer that you would give us pause when we feel disrespect in our heart or on our lips; knowing that it is not of you. Remove my disrespectful attitude and replace it with words and tone that are sweet like honeycomb. In Jesus' name. Amen.

*Let us respect
our managers
and our
colleagues as
God requires.*

READING TWENTY-FOUR

Reaching for Jesus

"In the morning, O Lord, You hear my voice; in the morning I lay my requests before You and wait in expectation." Psalm 5:3 (NIV)

WHEN we step into the office, anything can happen. Actually, as soon as we reach for our smartphone (which probably sits by the side of the bed) and scroll through our emails, we could find problems on the horizon, issues with projects, client concerns, and countless other issues. Before we reach for that smartphone, God wants us to reach for him. God wants us to go into our quiet place and spend time praying to him and then taking a few moments to be still and listen.

We know that we are heading off to a complicated world where anything can happen. Rather than leaving our day to chance, we should consider starting our day with God. Let's not let the day happen to us, but let us happen to the day. We should start each day giving God our concerns and praying over our interactions with colleagues, praying over the project costs that may be overrun, or praying over the client that seems to be disgruntled and difficult to please.

Dear God, we start our day with you. We start our day speaking to you, meditating on your word and then listening to your advice and direction. God, do not let our smartphone be the first communication that we have each day. Let that communication be with you. God, today we come to thank you for a restful night's sleep. We thank you for the beautiful day that you set before us. God, this morning, we ask you to bless our relationships with clients, coworkers, and managers. Today we ask that you would watch over our programs, budgets, and the human resources that we need to accomplish various tasks. God, we give them over to you today, expecting all to be well. We pray that you will cover them and that you will also cover us. Amen.

Rather than leaving our day to chance, we should consider starting our day with God.

READING TWENTY-FIVE

Safeguarding Your Day with God's Word

"Finally, be strong in the Lord and in his mighty power. Put on the full armor of God so that you can take your stand against the devil's schemes." Ephesians 6:10-11 (NIV)

NEWSFLASH – not only does the devil wear Prada, but the devil can also be in the office. Each day, we must put on the whole armor of God so that we do not fall prey to his schemes. The devil uses the office environment to shake us. He uses the stress of juggling multiple priorities to distract us from living in God's Word. Each day, prior to going into an environment that can be a playground for the devil, we should fill our mind with God's Word, and even keep reminders of the Scriptures surrounding us. Instead of a standard notepad for meeting notes, perhaps we could keep a journal with Scripture reminding us to not worry about tomorrow. Instead of a basic black coffee mug, perhaps we need a mug reminding us to be kind in the face of adversity. As the meeting discussions get intense or the project plan veers off schedule, those reminders will go a long way.

Dear Heavenly Father, today we are your warriors. We walk into our respective offices armed for battle; armed with the Word of truth. This morning, God, we have read your Word and placed it in our hearts so that just when we need it most, your word will be there. Help it come out of us in place of rudeness, offense, snide comments, or mediocrity. God, we pray that we will be slow to offense, we will speak kind words, and we will be excellent and never lazy. Thank you for providing the tools that we need to withstand what may occur today. God, we thank you that our spirit will not be moved. Amen.

Each day,
we must put
on the whole
armor of God
so that we do
not fall prey to
his schemes.

READING TWENTY-SIX

The Extra Mile

"We do not want you to become lazy, but to imitate those who through faith and patience inherit what has been promised." Hebrews 6:12 (NIV)

GOD does not like laziness. Such is the case in our professional work. Simply being in the office for the sake of being there is not God's way. In order to be excellent, we must aggressively seek to do a good job in all areas. We must start our day purposed, seek out new challenges, and refine the skills that we already have. To do anything other than that would be to be lazy; to do the minimum. If we work on a project team, perhaps we can ask business development how we can help to win new business in our area of expertise. If we are certified as a Project Management Professional, we can offer to host a class to help get our colleagues ready for the exam during lunch. It's all about going the extra mile.

God, we thank you today for encouraging us to seek after greatness. We seek after the prize of your heart as we seek to be excellent in business. We pray to be diligent and not lazy. Lord, dissolve anything in us that exhibits a spirit of laziness, and help us as we seek to do better. God, we pray to go the extra mile in our businesses in every area possible. Amen.

In order to be excellent, we must aggressively seek to do a good job in all areas.

READING TWENTY-SEVEN

Developing Perseverance while Starting New Ventures

"Consider it pure joy, my brothers, whenever you face trials of many kinds because you know that the testing of your faith develops perseverance." James 1:2-4 (NIV)

BEING a Christian in the business world is a great place to develop perseverance. Consider the faith to enter a new market with little to no organizational experience, competing with other new entrants that may have more experience and less costs. Consider the many disappointing moments losing bids, trying to sign clients, and establishing a reputation. The hard work requires dedication, and the dedication leads to perseverance. Throughout the trials of establishing this new business, do not be dismayed but consider it joy. Success will emerge.

Dear God, thank you for the hardships and trials of establishing a new business, a new line of business, and new operations. Thank you, God, that through these trials you are building our faith. Thank you for leading us in faith to continue until we persevere and succeed. God, we consider our trials pure joy, because you know that you will lead our new venture into success. We know that our trials will be many and the faith required will be great, but we pray to stay the course and stay positive in the faith of the future outcomes. God, bless our ventures. Bless all that we put our hands to do. Amen.

Throughout the trials of establishing this new business, do not be dismayed but consider it joy. Success will emerge.

READING TWENTY-EIGHT

Refine, Refine, Refine

"The end of a matter is better than its beginning and patience is better than pride." Ecclesiastes 7:8 (NIV)

PROPOSAL writing takes a lot of effort. Some people think that they can slap a proposal together in one or two drafts and be finished. God said that the final outcome should be better than how something starts out. This is absolutely true in proposal development. Proposals require iterations – many different revisions. There are many draft versions, then there is weaving in win themes and discriminators, and eventually a final copy. Proposal development means using every day of the process to refine, refine, refine. When we have 30 days to submit a proposal, we should use them. Wasting the first 20 days and then using the last 10 to develop a winning submission will most likely not lead to our desired outcome. This may take a lot of patience, but the outcome is worth it.

Dear God, thank you for giving us time to refine. Thank you for giving us patience and diligence to tirelessly work on developing a winning proposal. God, keep us from trying to cut the process short, and help us use every day of the proposal cycle to turn around a great product. God, we thank you that your Word is the crux of our proposal process and we employ your instruction. In Jesus' name we pray. Amen.

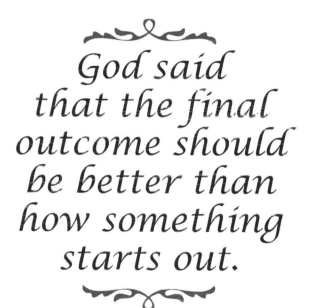

*God said
that the final
outcome should
be better than
how something
starts out.*

READING TWENTY-NINE

Managing Our Budgets

"He who is faithful in a very little thing is faithful also in much; and he who is unrighteous in a very little thing is unrighteous also in much." Luke 16:10 (New American Standard)

YEARS ago, when I received my first budget to manage, it was a small budget. When we start out, we want to manage large budgets, but we must first learn to manage the small ones. I remember wanting a resume bullet that said I managed multi-million dollar budgets, but God and my management needed to see that I could handle a small budget with accuracy and diligence. In our work, we must be faithful with the small budgets before we can graduate to the large ones. We must be able to take the small budgets and monitor them accurately, report up to management, run profit and loss statements, maintain company revenue, and of course ensure that budget does not run over. If we cannot handle managing a small budget; how can we pray and ask God to promote us to larger ones. As we show ourselves faithful in handling the small budget, God will continue to reward us with opportunities to manage the large budgets.

Dear God, we thank you for the opportunities that we have been given to prove ourselves. We thank you for the opportunity to manage the small things first. We thank you in advance, because we know that as we are faithful in the small things, you will bless us with the larger things. God, rather than looking to the big things, we will first focus on managing what you have given us. Amen.

As we show ourselves faithful in handling the small budget, God will continue to reward us with opportunities to manage the large budgets.

READING THIRTY

You are an Example

"Similarly, encourage the young men to be self-controlled. In everything set them an example by doing what is good. In your teaching show integrity and seriousness." Titus 2:6-7 (NIV)

AS we move through the ranks of our business, we set the standard and become role models for others. Sometimes this occurs through a formal or informal mentor relationship, a supervisory relationship, or even when someone completely unbeknownst to us is watching our behavior. These individuals admire our accomplishments and want to follow our path. We may not always know who is watching, but someone always is. Setting a good example for the less-seasoned team is not merely a nice thing to do; it is required by God.

Let us encourage the young people. Perhaps our organization does not have a formal mentor program. If not, adopt a newer professional and show them the way to thrive in business God's way. Teach them how simply using the fruit of the spirit can change the professional atmosphere and lead to both professional and spiritual success. Today, we commit to encouraging others to be self-controlled, by first exhibiting self-control, integrity, and dedication.

Dear God, thank you for another day to be a good example. Thank you, God, for giving us the opportunity to affect the lives of others positively. God, we pray that we would make the most of that opportunity daily. We pray to be salt and light to the younger men and women around us. God, we desire to show others in the office an example of you in all of our interactions. Guide us, guide our tongue, and order our actions. Amen.

We may
not always
know who
is watching,
but someone
always is.

ABOUT THE PUBLISHER

TheBiblePeople.com exists to help people read, understand, and apply the Bible.

Made in the USA
San Bernardino, CA
06 December 2018